HOW TO BE
A DOCTOR
AND OTHER LIVE-SAVING JOBS

Dream big and know that the power to make that dream come true, lies inside of you. I dedicate this book to the two people that taught me this and made me make my dreams come true . . . thank you Aarish and Ellora x
P.K.

To the best doctor (and my best friend) in the entire world, Dr. Carla Barbieri!
S.L.

First published 2022 by Nosy Crow Ltd
The Crow's Nest, 14 Baden Place, Crosby Row, London, SE1 1YW, UK

Nosy Crow Eireann Ltd, 44 Orchard Grove, Kenmare, Co Kerry, V93 FY22, Ireland

www.nosycrow.com

ISBN 978 1 83994 170 2 (HB)
ISBN 978 1 83994 232 7 (PB)

Nosy Crow and associated logos are trademarks
and/or registered trademarks of Nosy Crow Ltd

Text © Dr Punam Krishan 2022
Illustrations © Sol Linero 2022

The right of Dr Punam Krishan to be identified as the author
and Sol Linero to be identified as the illustrator of this work
has been asserted.

A CIP catalogue record for this book is available from the British Library.

Printed in China.

Papers used by Nosy Crow are made from wood grown in sustainable forests.

10 9 8 7 6 5 4 3 2 1 (HB)
10 9 8 7 6 5 4 3 2 1 (PB)

CONTENTS

WHAT IS A DOCTOR?

A doctor is someone whose job it is to look after sick people.

There are lots of different types of doctors to look after people of all ages, from new babies to the very elderly. They treat all kinds of **illnesses and conditions,** such as sore tummies, coughs, colds and broken bones, and they also discover **new medicines.**

Doctors work in various different places, including local surgeries, hospitals, laboratories and universities. They also occasionally visit unwell patients in their homes.

Wherever they work, doctors have to use special tools to help them find out what is wrong with the patient:

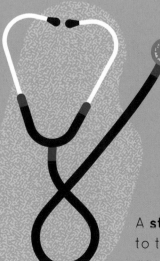

An **otoscope** to look into the patient's ears and throat.

A **stethoscope** to listen to the patient's heart as well as the lungs.

Taking care of a sick person, or a **patient,** is not an easy job, so doctors always need help. Doctors often work in teams with other **healthcare professionals,** such as . . .

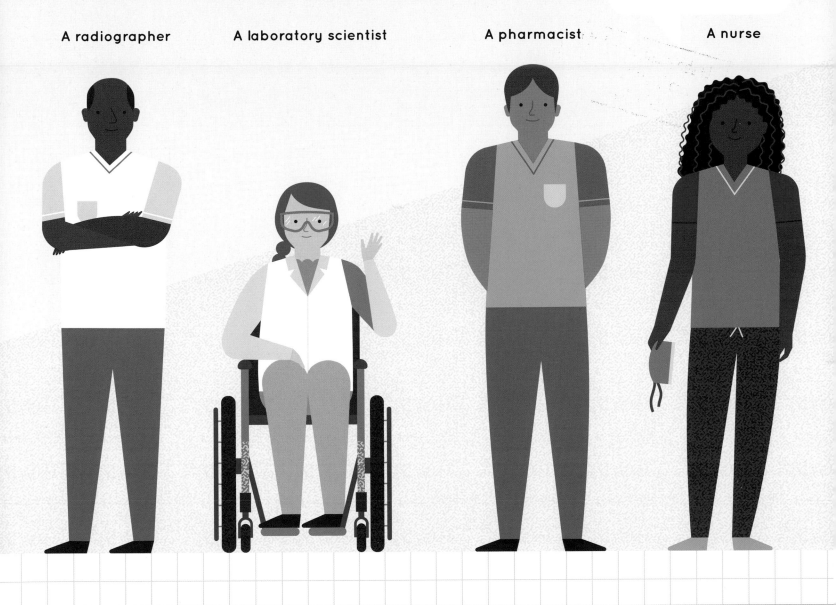

A radiographer   A laboratory scientist   A pharmacist   A nurse

An **ophthalmoscope** to look into the back of the patient's eyes.

A **pulse oximeter** to find out whether the patient is breathing in enough oxygen.

A **thermometer** to measure a person's temperature.
A person whose temperature is too hot might have an infection.

Once the doctor has all the information, they can use their knowledge and experience to tell the patient what the problem, or the **diagnosis**, is.

5

WHY DO WE NEED DOCTORS?

One hundred years ago, a person could expect to live to the age of around 50.

Thanks to science and doctors, people now live much longer and in better health. Today, the **average life expectancy** is between 75 and 80 years, though many people live even longer than this.

We need doctors because they **save thousands of lives every day.**

Doctors treat all kinds of illnesses, as well as helping people who have been seriously injured.

They also do check-ups on their patients and can often **stop an illness from developing** by catching it early and treating it before the illness causes any harm. Doctors also **discover new diseases** all the time and **find new cures.**

Sometimes doctors can give, or **prescribe,** a medicine that can help treat the problem. This might be a tablet or liquid that you swallow, or it might be a cream or an ointment to rub on your body.

Doctors also give **vaccinations,** which are a type of medicine that stops people from catching serious infections. In some cases, a doctor might need to do a **surgical operation,** which is when they have to fix something inside the patient's body using special tools.

People can become sick at any time of the day or night, but luckily doctors are **always there to help.** Doctors work long hours in **shifts** to make sure there is always a team to take care of anyone who needs help.

Often, **doctors themselves** can be a powerful medicine. If you feel sad or worried about anything, sharing this with a doctor can make you feel much better.

THE HISTORY OF
MEDICINE

For as long as humans have existed, illness and disease have been around, but over the past 2,500 years, doctors and scientists have worked hard to help treat and cure people.

The ancient Chinese emperor Huangdi is believed to have written a book about health and disease. Some of the treatments he wrote about are still being used today.

An ancient Greek doctor called Hippocrates started a medical school. Today, most doctors take the **Hippocratic Oath**, a promise to always be a good doctor.

Ignaz Semmelweis, a Hungarian doctor, discovered the importance of handwashing in medicine to stop the spread of germs.

| 2600 BC | 700 BC | 400 BC | 1796 | 1847 | 1849 |

Sushruta, an ancient Indian doctor, is believed to be the first to discover how to perform operations to cure diseases. His book is the oldest known medical textbook on surgery in the world.

Edward Jenner, a British surgeon, developed the first ever vaccine. It was used to stop people from getting smallpox, a virus that killed more than three million people across the world.

Elizabeth Blackwell was the first female **physician** (doctor) to be awarded a medical degree.

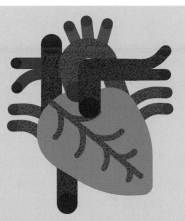

Mary Seacole and Florence Nightingale cared for hundreds of soldiers during the Crimean War. Florence Nightingale went on to set up the first school for nurses.

A Polish-French scientist called Marie Curie discovered **polonium** and **radium** which helped X-rays to take better pictures inside the human body. She was the first woman to win a Nobel prize.

A South African doctor called Christiaan Barnard was the first surgeon to perform a human heart transplant, a type of surgery that gives someone with a poorly heart a new, healthy heart.

| 1853–1856 | 1857 | 1898 | 1928 | 1967 | 2019 |

A French microbiologist called Louis Pasteur discovered germs and how they cause diseases. His work was hugely important in discovering treatments to infections caused by **bacteria** and viruses.

Sir Alexander Fleming, a Scottish doctor and microbiologist, discovered the first antibiotic, **Penicillin,** which has saved millions of lives and is still being used today.

A new type of **Coronavirus** called COVID-19 broke out, causing a worldwide **pandemic.**

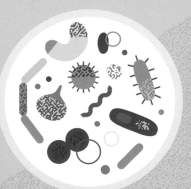

HOW DO YOU
BECOME A DOCTOR?

To become a doctor, you must be kind, caring, patient and curious. It is a job that involves working with lots of different people, so you need to enjoy talking to and spending time with others.

You also must be **interested in science** and enjoy **finding solutions to problems.** Even once you become a doctor, the learning never stops. Science is changing all the time, so doctors need to enjoy **studying** and **learning new things.**

To look after sick people, doctors must be good **team leaders,** but they also have to work with other healthcare professionals, so they need to be good at **working with others.**

There are lots of things you can do now to start training to become a doctor:

Spend time with an elderly relative or neighbour.

Join a local youth group such as the Cubs or Brownies to develop your teamwork skills.

Volunteer to help at a local food bank or charity.

Volunteer at a care home.

Talk to doctors, nurses or other healthcare professionals you meet and ask them about their job.

Find out if there are any first aid courses you can join.

DID YOU KNOW?
If you want to become a doctor, you should work hard at all subjects, but particularly science, maths and English.

Watch some science documentaries to learn more about the human body.

So, you are kind, curious and love learning new things and solving problems? You have all the right skills to become a doctor! But there's a lot of **training** to do first . . .

WHAT DO
DOCTORS NEED TO LEARN?

To study medicine, you need to work very hard at school in order to go to university. At university, doctors learn all about how the human body works and all the different medicines and ways to treat people.

To be a doctor you need to have a medical degree, which takes five to six years, but the learning does not stop there!

DID YOU KNOW?
Medical students practise special treatments on dummy bodies called **mannequins**.

After medical school, doctors have to **work in hospitals** to get more experience. For five to 15 years, they work as **junior doctors** across different areas of a hospital. During this time, they decide what type of doctor they would like to be – they may want to take care of sick children or become an eye doctor, for example. They have to **study hard** and take **lots of exams** in order to become experts.

Being a doctor is not an easy job. It can get very busy and doctors work long hours, which means they need to be good at **taking care of themselves as well as others.** If you want to become a doctor, you need to start taking good care of yourself by **eating well, exercising, getting enough sleep** and **finding hobbies** to relax.

Sadly, doctors can't always save everyone. Sometimes when people are very old or really poorly, they die. This is upsetting for everyone, especially the doctors, so you need to be able to **share your feelings** and **manage your emotions.** This is taught to medical students during their training and work experience.

After many years of training, it's time to decide which sort of doctor you would like to be.

WHAT HAPPENS WHEN
SOMEONE IS UNWELL?

When someone is feeling unwell, usually they will go for an appointment with their General Practitioner (GP).

GPs are family doctors. They treat all comon medical problems, and they have a very important role in teaching people about how to stay healthy and keep diseases away.

GPs see and treat people in many ways. They can see a patient in person, visit them at home, talk to them on the telephone or even speak to them over a video call.

DID YOU KNOW?
The creator of Sherlock Holmes, Sir Arthur Conan Doyle, was a GP. So was one of his characters, Dr Watson.

A GP might prescribe some medicine to the patient, or they might arrange for them to be seen by a specialist at a hospital. GPs work with many other key healthcare professionals who make up the **primary care team.**

The GP practice is a very busy place, but the **practice manager** helps it run smoothly by giving jobs to the right people.

Receptionists organise appointments for patients and speak to them when they arrive, as well as sending out letters and reports.

Physiotherapists help patients who have any injuries, illnesses or disabilities that could affect movement. They teach different exercises and may give patients special tools to help.

Cleaners work hard to ensure that the practice is clean and safe.

Phlebotomists take blood samples from patients and send them to the hospital where they can be analysed.

Porters collect all the samples doctors have taken from patients (blood, urine, poo) and take them to the hospital laboratories to be tested.

Practice nurses teach patients how to look after their health, give vaccinations, do tests, and some can even examine patients and prescribe medications.

After a doctor decides which medicine is needed, **pharmacists** safely check the medicine, make sure the right amount is given and package it up for the patient.

While most conditions can be managed by a GP, if someone is very unwell it is best to call an ambulance to take them to hospital.

THere Is A MedIcAl EMERGENCY?

A medical emergency is when someone needs care from a doctor straight away. If someone is hurt or needs help, they can phone 999 to speak to an emergency medical dispatcher. The dispatcher takes some important details and sends out the correct help.

EMERGENCY

If the person has to be taken to hospital, **paramedics** will drive to them very quickly in an **ambulance.** They are trained to help the patient at the scene and can perform life-saving treatments before taking them to the hospital.

DID YOU KNOW?

Some doctors and paramedics travel in helicopters to help people who need urgent medical help but can't be reached quickly or easily by ambulance.

The **Accident and Emergency department** is the first place of treatment in hospitals for patients with **injuries or serious illnesses.** There are lots of doctors who work there and are trained to deal with a wide range of medical issues. You can never predict what emergency will come in next, so the teams are always ready.

People can also go to
the hospital themselves.

It is often very loud and
busy in the emergency
department and everyone
working there has an
essential role to play ...

The **receptionists** ask questions about
the patient and passes this information
to the nurses and doctors.

Healthcare assistants help by checking
a patient's 'vital signs', which include
blood pressure, temperature, weight,
height and oxygen levels, and they may
also need to do a blood or urine test.

A **triage nurse**
checks how
serious the
problem is and
how quickly you
need to be seen
by the doctor.

Radiographers
work near
the emergency
department and
give X-rays or
scans to see what
is happening
inside people's
bodies.

WHAT HAPPENS WHEN SOMEONE
NEEDS AN OPERATION?

Sometimes patients may need an operation. The emergency doctors work closely with other specialist doctors who can perform the life-saving surgeries.

Most operations are planned ahead of time – for example, if someone keeps getting a sore throat, they might need to have their tonsils taken out. But if there has been a medical emergency, a person may need to have an operation immediately.

Vascular surgeons know all about how your blood travels around the body.

Urological surgeons look after the organs that help you to wee properly.

Paediatric surgeons do operations on children who are poorly, from babies born very early to teenagers.

Neurosurgeons operate on the brain and spine.

Oral and Maxillofacial surgeons treat problems with the mouth, jaw, face and neck.

Plastic surgeons can minimise scars and even create new skin for people with serious burns.

Orthopaedic surgeons fix nasty broken bones.

Ear Nose and Throat surgeons treat diseases of the head and neck, but mainly the ears, nose and throat.

DID YOU KNOW?
In order to keep everyone safe from infections during an operation, everyone in the operating theatre must wear special clothing including masks, hats, gloves, gowns and shoes.

To be a surgeon, you need to have excellent **hand-eye coordination,** as well as lots of energy, because some operations can take many hours. Surgeons must be able to **work with others** but also be reliable **team leaders.** They have to be great **problem solvers,** always ready to react if things don't go to plan.

Anaesthetists may need to put the patient to sleep depending on the operation, but at all times they keep a close eye to make sure the patient is not in any pain and that their heart and breathing are working well. They have special medicines to keep the patient comfortable throughout the surgery.

Cardiothoracic surgeons fix problems with the heart and lungs and can even replace poorly hearts with new ones.

99
90
120/80

WHAT HAPPENS WHEN
SOMEONE HAS A BABY?

Some people choose to have their babies at home, but most have their babies in a hospital. When a person is pregnant, they are looked after by a very important group of doctors called the antenatal team.

The **midwife** is an expert in pregnancies and births. Giving birth to a baby is hard work and midwives are there to give support and care. They monitor the pregnant person throughout their pregnancy and help during the birth to safely bring their baby into the world. Most babies, whether born at home or in a hospital, are delivered with the help of a midwife alone.

DID YOU KNOW?
Nearly 400,000 babies are born every day in the world!

Sometimes things can go wrong and the pregnant person may need emergency treatment or help. This is when the midwife will call a doctor specially trained in pregnancy and birth, called an **obstetrician,** to help. These doctors can do various important and life-saving treatments and surgeries to make sure the pregnant person remains well and that the baby arrives safely.

Anaesthetists use different types of medicines to make giving birth less painful. For those who may need an operation to get the baby out safely, anaesthetists may give special injections to make the area numb so it doesn't hurt. They also keep a close eye on both the pregnant person and baby throughout the birth.

Some babies are born **premature,** which means that they arrive early, so they may need to stay in hospital for some time until they are strong and healthy.

They are taken care of in the **neonatal unit** by **neonatologists** who have special training in looking after premature and unwell babies.

Paediatricians are doctors who care for babies and children. They are usually called if there is a problem when the baby is being born, and they always come to check the baby over to make sure they are healthy and safe to go home.

WHO LOOKS AFTER OLDER PEOPLE?

As adults get older, their bodies change which means they often need extra care and attention.

Older people might have problems moving around or with their balance, which can make them fall over, or they might have problems with their heart and other organs, which can require lots of medicines. Older people can also become more forgetful.

A **big specialist team** of people take care of not just the medical problems, but also how older people are feeling.

These doctors need to be good at **talking and listening** to their patients, as well as being **respectful and patient.** They want to keep their patients as **healthy** as possible, giving them all the help and support they need.

DID YOU KNOW?
People are living longer than ever before. The oldest person alive today is 118 years old!

Geriatricians are doctors who treat conditions that affect older adults. They take care of complicated health problems when patients are in hospital and also visit them at their local doctor's surgery.

Occupational therapists teach older patients with problems moving their bodies how to do everyday tasks that they might struggle with, like getting dressed, climbing stairs, having a bath and eating.

Social workers look after the needs of the elderly, from helping them find suitable places to live to how they manage their money.

They can organise for people to clean their houses and to prepare and deliver their food or even do their shopping, as well as making sure our older adults are feeling safe and well.

District nurses visit older patients in their homes or care homes to check their blood pressure, do blood tests, check any wounds that need to be dressed, give injections and make sure they are happy.

ARE YOU INTERESTED IN

THE WAY PEOPLE THINK?

THEN ONE OF THESE JOBS MIGHT BE FOR YOU.

The brain is a very powerful and important part of our body. It doesn't just control what we think, it also controls how we feel.

Sometimes thoughts and feelings can become too much and make someone feel worried, stressed or very sad. There are lots of different **mental health experts** who are trained to help children and adults feel happier and healthier. These experts must be very **friendly, patient** and **good at listening and speaking** to their patients.

Psychiatrists are doctors who lead and work with other mental health experts. They can diagnose mental illnesses and prescribe medicines or other treatments, such as counselling and therapy.

Counsellors and **therapists** help people to talk about their feelings and see things more clearly or in a different way.

Psychologists spend time talking to people and helping them to understand their thoughts, feelings and behaviour.

Child psychologists might give children toys to play with while they talk.

Neuropsychologists are psychologists who work with people that have (or might have) brain illnesses or injuries. They must be experts in the brain, spinal cord and all the nerves in the body.

They use special machines to do **MRI scans** which produce images of the brain.

Mental health nurses work in hospitals and in people's homes to help support patients who are recovering from mental health problems.

Peer support workers use their own experiences of mental health problems to help other people who are receiving mental health treatments.

DID YOU KNOW?
Eating well, exercising and having a good night's sleep can help to improve your mental health.

DO YOU LIKE DOING

SCIENCE EXPERIMENTS?
THEN ONE OF THESE JOBS MIGHT BE FOR YOU.

Doctors sometimes need help from medical scientists before they can treat a patient. A medical scientist is a bit like a detective – they have to be curious, pay close attention to detail and be very good at solving problems.

If germs, like viruses or bacteria, get inside someone's body and make them ill, this is called an infection. In order to give the patient the right medication, doctors need to know which germ has caused it. **Microbiologists** are experts in finding germs. Using a microscope, they examine a patient's wee, spit, blood, poo and sometimes even fluid from their spine.

Infection is one cause of disease, but there can be others too. If a doctor thinks there might be something wrong with a patient's blood, they can send a sample to a laboratory to be examined by **haematologists** who can identify any problems.

A doctor might also send samples of a patient's blood or other samples taken from a patient to **clinical biochemists.** They help to diagnose and manage diseases by studying the chemicals in a patient's body.

Pathologists are experts in diseases. They use microscopes to study the cells and tissues inside their patients' bodies. Some pathologists examine people's bodies after they have died to find out what made them sick. This is a good way to learn more about diseases and how to stop them.

Doctors need **pharmacists** to help them give patients the right medicine. Some work in local pharmacies, doctor's surgeries or hospitals. Others work for companies that make medicines, or as part of research teams that discover new medicines.

There is still a lot to find out about medicine and diseases. **Medical research scientists** work in many different places, from science labs to universities. Their job is to investigate and come up with new ways to help stop diseases.

DID YOU KNOW?
There are more connections between the cells in your brain than there are stars in the Milky Way.

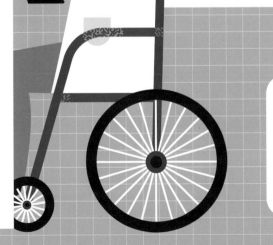

WHAT ABOUT THE MORE
UNUSUAL LIFE-SAVING JOBS?

If you love sports and science, then maybe you could become a **sports doctor.** They help professional sports people such as footballers, gymnasts and rugby players if they become injured, and support their mental and physical health during training.

If you like travelling and exploring new places, you could become an **expedition doctor.** They look after explorers and researchers in extreme parts of the world, such as Mount Everest, the Antarctic and the Sahara Desert.

The army, navy and air force need **military doctors** in case anyone becomes unwell. They might be based at a camp nearby or they might travel with the military team. They see all sorts of medical problems and must act quickly in an emergency.

Forensic doctors investigate crime scenes and find out what happened to people who died. Their expert knowledge helps police, detectives and lawyers to solve crimes.

Media doctors work on TV shows and report on health issues in the news. They give advice on the radio and TV, take part in podcasts and YouTube videos, and even write books like this one.

Space doctors keep astronauts and space crew fit and healthy as they travel through the solar system.

Some doctors travel to countries in trouble as part of organisations like **Médicins Sans Frontières (Doctors Without Borders).** They help to save people caught in wars or natural disasters like bush fires, hurricanes and floods.

29

WHAT HAPPENS WHEN THERE IS A
WORLD HEALTH CRISIS?

When an infectious disease spreads to lots of people and causes an epidemic or a pandemic, we need experts to find out about the virus that caused the disease, who is at risk, how to stop it spreading and how to make sure it never happens again.

Public health specialists look after the health of a whole group of people rather than individual patients. They work hard to find new ways to improve the health of communities and stop diseases.

DID YOU KNOW?
An epidemic is when a disease spreads in just one area. A pandemic is when it spreads across several countries. An infectious disease called COVID-19 caused a worldwide pandemic in 2020.

Epidemiologists investigate diseases that spread quickly in groups of people. By gathering and studying lots of information, they find out how diseases start and how they pass from one person to another. They can then advise doctors, scientists and even the government on how to control the spread of these diseases.

Volunteers help in hospitals and care homes, work for charities, test new medicines for scientists and help out the people most at risk from catching the disease.

Virologists are experts in diagnosing infections caused by viruses. During epidemics and pandemics, they work closely with public health specialists and epidemiologists to find out how the virus spreads.

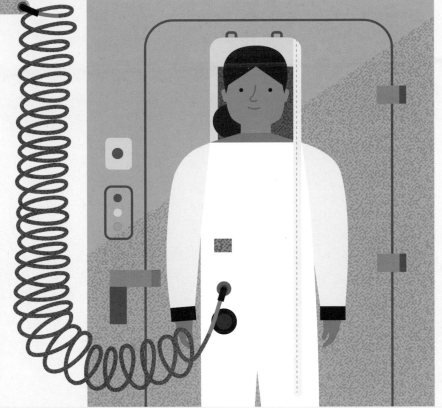

Immunologists work in teams to develop new treatments or vaccines to control diseases.

The **Chief Medical Officer** is the most senior doctor in a country. They advise the government on health issues affecting people in that country.

Many experts around the world work for the **World Health Organisation.** Together, they stop diseases spreading and keep the world safe and healthy.

Healthcare jobs have never been more important. Doctors, scientists and other medical professionals work hard to stop pandemics and save billions of lives every day. Maybe one day **you** will be a life-saver too!

GET INVOLVED!

If you would like to learn more about becoming a doctor or saving lives, there are many things you can do . . .

Have a chat with any doctors, nurses or healthcare professionals that you might know or visit and ask them more about their jobs. Later down the line, you could even organise to do some work experience with them.

You can also get in touch with a local care home to ask about any volunteering opportunities, join a local science club to learn more about medicine and the human body, go on a junior first aid course, help out at a soup kitchen for the homeless and spend time with an elderly relative or neighbour.

To begin with, all you really need is a passion for helping people and saving lives!

USEFUL ORGANISATIONS AND WEBSITES INCLUDE:

Youth Programmes at St John Ambulance https://youthjoining.sja.org.uk/
The Brownies https://www.girlguiding.org.uk/what-we-do/brownies-7-10
The Cubs https://www.scouts.org.uk/cubs/
Operation Ouch! https://www.bbc.co.uk/cbbc/shows/operation-ouch
Terrific Scientific https://www.bbc.co.uk/teach/terrific-scientific
Wow Science https://wowscience.co.uk/